VISIONS
A N D
DREAMS

COURAGE FOR TODAY. HOPE FOR THE FUTURE.

Also by Jack Blanco:

The Clear Word
The Clear Word for Kids
The Clear Word Psalms and Proverbs
The Clear Word—The Gospel of John
The Easy English Clear Word
Savior: Four Gospels. One Story.

To order, call 1-800-765-6955.

Visit us at www.AutumnHousePublishing.com for information on other Autumn House® products.

A Fresh Look at Daniel and Revelation

VISIONS
AND
DREAMS

COURAGE FOR TODAY. HOPE FOR THE FUTURE.

JACK BLANCO

Autumn
House® Publishing
www.autumnhousepublishing.com
A Division of REVIEW AND HERALD® PUBLISHING
Since 1861

Published by Autumn House® Publishing, a division of Review and Herald° Publishing, Hagerstown, MD 21741-1119

This book was
Edited by Steven S. Winn
Copyedited by James Cavil
Cover designed by Trent Truman
Interior designed by Johanna Macomber
Cover photo: © istockphoto.com/ooyoo; candle illustration by William Hutchinson
        © Review and Herald Publishing Association, Hagerstown, MD
Typeset: Bembo 12/14

PRINTED IN U.S.A.

14 13 12 11 10   5 4 3 2 1

Library of Congress Cataloging-in-Publication Data
Blanco, Jack J., 1929-   .
  Visions and dreams : hope for the future, courage for today : a fresh look at Daniel and Revelation / Jack Blanco.
      p. cm.
    1. Bible. O.T. Daniel—Prophecies. 2. Bible. O.T. Daniel—Criticism, interpretation, etc. 3. Bible. N.T. Revelation—Prophecies. 4. Bible. N.T. Revelation—Criticism, interpretation, etc. 5. End of the world—Biblical teaching. 6. End of the world—Prophecies. I. Title.
    BS1556.B53 2009
    220'.046—dc22

                                        2009014527
ISBN 978-0-8127-0478-5

To all those
longing for God's kingdom,
and to Jesus Christ,
who has filled our hearts with hope.

Contents

Note to Reader . . .

This conversational paraphrase of the prophecies of Daniel and Revelation from Scripture is grouped into 10 short, easy, readable chapters. In Daniel the chapters are grouped according to Daniel's life experiences. In Revelation the chapters are grouped according to John's visions. The Scripture references are given at various points throughout each reading.

The prophecies of Daniel and Revelation are the most extensive prophecies in Scripture. Daniel was written hundreds of years before Christ, pointing to the Messiah's life and death and on to His ascension and ministry before God in the heavenly sanctuary. The apostle John's visions expand the view of Christ's ministry and provide insights into the spiritual struggles of God's people through the centuries, ending with the second coming of Christ and the creation of a new heaven and a new earth.

The reading of these prophecies gives hope for the future and courage for the present, through the continued ministry of Christ before God on behalf of His people and against the wickedness and violence in this world. His promise is that the time will come when there will be no more sorrow, pain, sickness, death, or crying. He will make all things new.

May this conversational reading of the prophecies lead the reader into a deeper study of these prophetic books. As Jesus told John: "These words are true and faithful."

For the glory and praise of Jesus Christ,
Jack J. Blanco

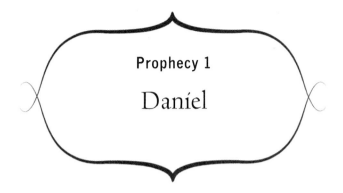

Prophecy 1

Daniel

Captives in Babylon

After Jehoiakim, king of Judah, was made to submit to the king of Babylon for three years, he rebelled against him. So Nebuchadnezzar invaded the land, surrounded Jerusalem, and took Jehoiakim prisoner, as well as many others. Nebuchadnezzar decided to take the treasures of the Temple and many of its items to Babylon to be placed in the temple of his god. But he had to hurry back because of his father's death, so he gave Ashpenaz the responsibility of seeing that the prisoners and the treasures of Jerusalem were brought to Babylon.

When the captives arrived, Nebuchadnezzar asked Ashpenaz to select from the captives young men of royal descent who would be educated and trained to serve in the palace. Those selected were to be physically well built, handsome, intelligent, self-disciplined, and quick to learn. They were to receive special treatment and be served the same menu as those who ate at the king's table.

Among the Hebrew captives chosen were four young men: Daniel, Hananiah, Mishael, and Azariah. Their names were changed to Belteshazzar, Shadrach, Meshach, and Abednego, identifying them as servants of the gods of Babylon.

Daniel had made up his mind not to eat the meat or drink the wine that was served. So he asked Ashpenaz for permission to have a simple Hebrew diet. Ashpenaz loved Daniel and was kind to him, but he said, "If I grant your request and the king sees that you're not as healthy as the other students and finds out that I changed your diet, I'll be executed."

Then Daniel talked to Melzar, who was directly in charge of him and his three friends, and said, "Try us on a Hebrew diet of vegetables and water for 10 days and see if we don't look healthier than the other students. If we look sickly or don't do as well as they do, then you can make your decision, and whatever you decide, we'll do."

Melzar agreed to let them try it. At the end of 10 days Daniel and his friends looked healthier and did better than the students who had eaten the king's meat and drunk his wine. So Melzar allowed them to stay on their Hebrew diet.

As Daniel and his friends went through their studies, God blessed them and gave them wisdom and skill in every subject. And He gave Daniel the ability to interpret visions and dreams.

When the three-year course was over, the chief official took all the students to the king for their final exam. Nebuchadnezzar questioned each of them and found that Daniel and his three friends did much better than any of the others. The king was so impressed that he made them members of his royal court. He also found that their answers and advice were 10 times better than those of the astrologers, fortune tellers, and priests.

Daniel served the kings of Babylon for years, even until Cyrus the Persian conquered Babylon and established the Medo-Persian Empire (Dan. 1).

The King's Dream

After Nebuchadnezzar had completed his inaugural year and had been in office for two years, he had a dream that really bothered him. There were parts of it that he couldn't put together, and it troubled him so much that he couldn't sleep. First thing in the morning he called together the experienced astrologers, fortune tellers, and priests, who claimed to talk with the dead, and asked them to explain the dream.

He said to them, "I had a dream last night that troubles me. I'm really concerned about it. I couldn't sleep well most of the night. I need to know what it means."

His advisers replied, "Tell us the dream, Your Majesty, and we'll tell you what it means."

The king said, "I can't remember the dream. That's what bothers me, and that's why I called you together. I need your help. If you don't tell me the dream and its meaning, I'll have you all killed and will turn your houses into a dump site. If you do tell me the dream and interpret it for me, I'll reward each of you handsomely and honor you throughout my kingdom."

They answered, "Your Majesty, tell us the dream and we'll interpret it for you."

The king responded, "Are you telling me that you can't tell me what I dreamed last night? Are you stalling for time? If you can't tell me the dream, how would I know that your interpretation is correct and that you're not just lying to me? Then all the powers you claim you have must be false, so how can I trust the other advice you've given me? You had better tell me the dream!"

The advisers became fearful and said, "Your Majesty, no one can tell another man what he dreamed, and no king has ever demanded such a thing. No one can know what someone else dreamed except the gods, but they don't live here."

Nebuchadnezzar was furious! He ordered all his advisers killed, including those who had just graduated, which included Daniel and his three friends. The death decree was written up, the king signed it, and the royal guards went through the city to arrest all the advisers and bring them to the king.

When Arioch, the captain in charge of the king's guards, came to arrest Daniel and his three friends, Daniel asked, "Why did the king issue such a harsh decree so quickly? That's not like him. There must be something terribly wrong." Arioch told him what had happened. Then Daniel asked for permission to go and see the king immediately, and the captain let him go.

Daniel hurried in to see Nebuchadnezzar and asked him for an extension, promising to tell him the dream and interpret it for him. The king agreed.

Then Daniel rushed back to his three friends and told them that the king had given them a short time to come up with the dream and its meaning. They prayed as they had never prayed before, asking God to help them or they would be killed along with all the other advisers. That night God gave Daniel the same dream He had given to Nebuchadnezzar and explained the meaning.

In the morning Daniel got up and said, "Praise the God of heaven forever and ever. All wisdom and power are His. He controls times, years, and seasons. He sets up kings and removes kings.

VISIONS AND DREAMS

He gives wisdom, insight, and understanding. He reveals mysteries and knows what man can't know. He is the source of all knowledge and floods the world with light. O Lord, my God, I thank You and praise You for what You have shown me. You gave me courage to go and see the king and then gave me insight into the meaning of his dream. You have answered our prayers. Now I can go and help the king."

Then Daniel went to see Arioch, the captain of the guard, and said to him, "You don't have to carry out the king's command to kill his advisers. I'm ready to tell the king his dream and interpret it for him."

So Arioch took Daniel to the king and said, "Your Majesty, I have found someone among the Jewish captives who can tell you the dream and interpret it for you."

The king asked Daniel, "Can you tell me the dream and interpret it?"

Daniel answered, "Your Majesty, no philosopher, astrologer, fortune teller, or priest can do that. But there is a God in heaven who knows everything and can explain all mysteries. Let me tell you the dream and interpret it for you. This is not because of any wisdom that I have. My friends and I prayed, and the God of heaven gave me the same dream that you had and told me what it means.

"Before you went to sleep, you were worried about the future of Babylon. So during the night God showed you the future all the way to the end of time. In your dream you saw an enormous statue of a man. It was so huge it was frightening. Its head was made of gold, its chest and arms of silver, its waist and hips of bronze, its legs of iron, and its feet were a mixture of iron and clay.

"After that you saw a large stone break loose from a mountain without help, come flying through the air toward the statue, strike its feet, and crush it to pieces. When the huge statue fell over, the stone rolled over it, grinding all the metals to powder. Then a wind came and blew it all away. Next you saw the stone get bigger and bigger, until it became a mountain and filled the whole earth.

"This is what you dreamed, Your Majesty. Now let me interpret it for you. You are represented by the head of gold. The God of heaven has given you the kingdom of Babylon. You are a king of kings. He has given you a mighty army, power to rule, and great honor and respect among the nations.

"But another kingdom will come and replace yours. It will be great in scope, but inferior, just as silver is inferior to gold. This kingdom will be replaced by another kingdom, which will be still greater in scope, but inferior still, just as bronze is inferior to silver.

"The fourth kingdom will be a kingdom of iron. Its scope will be greater than the others, but it will be even more inferior, just as iron is inferior to bronze. It will crush all opposition, just as iron can crush these other metals. This kingdom will eventually break up into 10 parts, represented by the toes. But just as iron and clay do not bond, the relationship among these kingdoms will sometimes be strong and sometimes weak. The kings will try to hold things together by intermarriage, but it won't work, just as iron can't stick to clay.

"That's when the God of heaven will come and set up His kingdom. It will destroy all the kingdoms and will last forever. God's kingdom is represented by the stone you saw break off from the mountain, hit the statue on its feet, grind the metals to powder, and grow into a huge mountain that filled the earth. With this, God is telling you ahead of time what will happen in the future. This is the dream, Your Majesty, and its meaning."

Then Nebuchadnezzar stood up, bowed to Daniel, and ordered sacrifices and incense to be offered to the God of heaven. He said to Daniel, "Your God is above all other gods. He is Lord of lords and King of kings. He alone knows the future and can explain mysteries."

The king rewarded Daniel for what he had done, gave him many gifts, and put him in charge of all the advisers. He also made him governor of the province of Babylon, which included the city. At Daniel's request the king appointed Shadrach, Meshach, and Abednego to be administrators in his kingdom (Dan. 2).

Prophecy 2

The King Changes

As time went on, Nebuchadnezzar gradually changed. He became proud and built a statue like the one he had seen in his dream years before. It was about 100 feet high, 10 feet wide, and all gold (not just its head). Nebuchadnezzar wanted to make a statement that the kingdom of Babylon would last forever. He set the statue up on the plain of Dura outside Babylon.

After the huge statue was set up, the king invited all the advisers, administrators, treasurers, governors, judges, magistrates, and representatives from other nations for the dedication. When they all got there, the king's spokesman announced in a loud voice: "People of nations, languages, and races, welcome to the dedication. When the trumpets sound and the music begins, the great king of Babylon wants you to declare your loyalty to him and the kingdom by bowing down and worshipping this great statue he has built. Those who refuse will be thrown into the nearby blazing furnace that the king has ordered to be heated up."

When the trumpets sounded, everyone bowed down—everyone, that is, except Shadrach, Meshach, and Abednego. Those who saw these men standing went to the king and said, "Your Majesty, there are some Jews who have refused to declare loyalty to you and Babylon. They have not bowed down to the statue as you told us to."

The king flew into a rage and ordered his guards to bring the three men to him at once. When they got there, he said to them, "Is it true that you men have refused to declare your loyalty to me and Babylon by not bowing down to the golden image I set up? I'll give you one more chance. As soon as the trumpets sound and the music begins, I want you to face the golden statue and bow down to it. If you refuse, I'll have you thrown into the fiery furnace, and no one will be able to save you."

The three Hebrews answered, "Your Majesty, it is true. We didn't bow down to the statue, because our first loyalty is to the God of heaven. He is able to deliver us. But even if He does not, we will not bow down to this golden statue."

Nebuchadnezzar was furious and ordered the furnace to be heated up seven times hotter. Then he asked his guards to throw the three men into the fire. So they tied them up and threw them into the blazing furnace, clothes and all. Some of the guards got too close to the flames, and they burned to death. The three Hebrews landed in the furnace fully dressed—robes, turbans, and all—tied hand and foot.

Suddenly Nebuchadnezzar jumped up and said to his officials nearby, "Look! Didn't we throw three men into the fire?"

They answered, "Yes, Your Majesty."

He said, "But I see four men in there walking around as if nothing had happened! And the fourth one looks like the Son of God that they told me about!"

Then the king went over to the furnace and called out, "Shadrach! Meshach! Abednego! Come out of there!"

The three young men walked out, and the officials gathered around to take a good look at them. They saw that their bodies were not burned, not a hair was singed, and their robes didn't even smell of smoke.

Then the king said, "Praise the God of Shadrach, Meshach, and Abednego! He sent His Son as an angel of heaven to rescue these men. They are so loyal that they were willing to risk their lives for Him! Therefore, I make this decree: Anyone who speaks against the God of heaven will be cut to pieces and his house turned into a dump site. No other god can save like this!"

Then Nebuchadnezzar promoted Shadrach, Meshach, and Abednego to even higher positions in the province of Babylon than they had before (Dan. 3).

The King's Second Dream

About a year later God gave Nebuchadnezzar a second dream that Daniel had to interpret for him. The king wrote this account of what happened: "May peace be multiplied to people, languages, and nations everywhere. Let me tell you the miracles the God of heaven did for me personally. How mighty are His works! His kingdom is an everlasting kingdom, and He rules for ever and ever.

"I was at peace in my palace, enjoying the greatness and splendor of Babylon. Then I had a dream that frightened me, and I couldn't go back to sleep. So in the morning I called together the wise men of Babylon—the experienced astrologers, magicians, fortune tellers, and priests—to interpret the dream for me, but they couldn't. So I called for Daniel and asked him to interpret it for me.

"When he came, I said, 'Daniel, I know that the Spirit of God is in you and that there is no mystery that you can't explain. I had a dream that really troubled me. In this dream I saw a huge tree. As I looked, it grew bigger and bigger, until it looked as if it were touching the sky. Everyone in the world could see this tree. Its leaves were beautiful, and it was loaded with fruit. Birds built their nests in it, and animals of all kinds came and rested in its shade.

" 'Then I saw a Holy Watcher come down from heaven in the form of an angel who said to those with Him, "Cut down the tree. Strip off its leaves. Scatter its fruit. Drive the birds and animals away. But leave the stump and roots in the ground. Put a band of iron and bronze around it and let it stay in the field. Then take away the reason of the man whom this tree represents and let him live in the field as an animal for seven years. This has been decided by the God of heaven, who keeps a watchful eye on all human affairs. He gives kingdoms to whomever He wills and sets over them the most common of men."

" 'This is the dream I had. Now tell me what it means. All my advisers and the wise men of Babylon could not interpret it for me. But I know you can because the Spirit of God is in you.'

"Daniel was so stunned by what he had heard that he stood speechless. I waited, then I spoke, 'Daniel, don't be afraid to tell me what the dream means. I want to know.'

"Finally, Daniel said, 'Your Majesty, how I wish the dream would apply to your enemies, but it doesn't. The tree that you saw with its leaves and fruit to which the birds and animals came represents you. The God of heaven has blessed you, and your kingdom has grown and is admired by people everywhere.

Prophecy 2: The King Changes

" 'The Holy Watcher commanded that the tree be cut down, but that the stump be left in the field with an iron and bronze band. This decision concerns you, Your Majesty. Your reason will be taken from you, and you will have the mind of an animal. Your officials will drive you out of the palace, and you will live in the field and eat grass like an ox. You will live that way for seven years until in your heart you know that God rules the world and gives the kingdom to whomever He will. Just as the stump remains, your kingdom will remain.

" 'Therefore, Your Majesty, stop sinning, do what's right, and be merciful to the poor and needy. Perhaps this will defer the sentence, and you will continue to prosper.' "

One year later, as Nebuchadnezzar was walking on the roof of his palace overlooking the city of Babylon, he said, "Just look at that! I'm the one who built this great city, and I did it as a showcase of my power and for the glory of my name."

No sooner did the words leave his mouth than a voice from heaven spoke: "Nebuchadnezzar! I am taking the kingdom away from you. Your reason is now gone, and your officials will drive you out of the palace and let you live in the field like an animal for seven years. Then you will know that God rules in the kingdom of men and has given you everything you have."

And that's exactly what happened. Nebuchadnezzar lost his reason and was taken from the palace to live in the fields for seven years. He ate grass like an ox. His hair grew as long as eagle feathers, and his nails looked like the claws of a bird.

At the end of the seven years the king's reason returned, and he looked up to heaven and said, "Blessed be the Most High God who lives forever. All praise and honor go to Him. His kingdom is an everlasting kingdom. People of the earth are as nothing compared to the universe. He commands the armies of heaven. No one can stand up against Him or question what He does.

"My counselors, advisers, and officials came looking for me and gave me back my throne and kingdom. So now, I, Nebuchadnezzar, king of Babylon, praise the God of heaven and honor the King of kings, who is just and does what is right. He humbles those who are proud and powerful" (Dan. 4).

Prophecy 3

A New King

After Nebuchadnezzar died, his son-in-law, Nabonidus, and his son, Belshazzar, shared the throne. One day Belshazzar decided to have a New Year's feast with 1,000 lords and noblemen and their wives. As they ate and drank together, Belshazzar asked his servants to bring in the gold and silver cups from the Temple in Jerusalem that Nebuchadnezzar had brought to Babylon. After the drinking vessels were brought in, everyone drank from them as they praised the gods of gold and silver who had made Babylon great.

Suddenly a human hand appeared high up on the wall and began writing where the lamps stood. Belshazzar turned pale, his knees began to shake, and he cried out for someone to bring in the magicians, astrologers, fortune tellers, and priests to interpret the writing. When they came, he said to them, "Anyone who can tell me the meaning of what is written on the wall I will dress in royal purple, put a golden chain around his neck, and make him third in power after my father and me."

The wisest men in Babylon all tried, but they could not come up with the meaning. Belshazzar felt sick. He didn't know what to do, and neither did his guests.

When the queen mother heard that the celebration had stopped, she came in to see what had happened. She saw the handwriting on the wall and said, "Your Majesty, don't be so terrified! Don't look so pale! There is someone who can interpret the writing for you. His name is Daniel. The Spirit of the God of heaven is in him. He interpreted mysteries for your grandfather that the wise men couldn't. I would suggest you send for him, and he will interpret it for you."

So Daniel was brought in, and Belshazzar asked, "Are you the Daniel who was brought here as one of the captives from Jerusalem and who interpreted mysteries for my grandfather? I have heard that you did. If you can interpret the handwriting on the wall, I will dress you in royal purple, put a gold chain around your neck, and make you third in power in the kingdom."

Daniel answered, "I don't need gifts, Your Majesty. I'll be happy to interpret the words for you. The God of heaven made your grandfather king of Babylon and gave him power and great glory. Nations stood in awe of him. Whatever he wanted to do he did, whether it was to execute someone or let him live. But when he became proud, God took away his reason, and he was driven from the palace and lived in the field, eating grass like an animal for seven years. When he came to himself and acknowledged that the God of heaven rules in the kingdom of men, God gave him back his reason and his throne.

"But you have not humbled yourself as your grandfather did, even though you knew this. You brought in holy vessels from the Temple in Jerusalem, drank from them, and worshipped the gods of gold and silver. You showed no respect for the God of heaven who holds your breath in His hand. That's why He sent this hand to write these three words on the wall.

" 'MENE, MENE' is repeated because of its certainty, and it means that the days of your kingdom are numbered. 'TEKEL' means that you have been weighed in the scales of heaven and found to be lacking. 'UPHARSIN' is in the plural and means that your kingdom has been given to the Medes and the Persians."

Then Belshazzar put a royal purple robe on Daniel, hung a golden chain on his neck, and announced that Daniel was third in power in the kingdom.

That same night the Persians under Cyrus took the city, killed Belshazzar, and placed Cyrus's 62-year old uncle, Darius the Mede, on the throne while Cyrus led his army on to conquer the rest of the kingdom (Dan. 5).

The Lions' Den

When Darius took over, he decided to appoint 120 governors to help rule the kingdom. Then he appointed three vice regents to whom the governors were responsible, and made Daniel head of the other two.

Daniel was very capable and stood out from the others by his administrative ability, so much so that the old king considered using him to help manage the whole kingdom. When the other two vice regents and the governors heard this, they decided to find something wrong with the way Daniel handled things, but they couldn't. So they focused on his religion.

They went to the king and said, "Your Majesty, as we look at our responsibilities governing your great kingdom, we feel that it would be easier if, at the beginning of your reign, you would make a decree testing the loyalty of your people. For at least 30 days no one should petition any god or man, except you, for anything. Whoever does should be thrown into the lions' den."

Darius thought that was a good idea, so he wrote it up and signed it into law. And according to the Medes and Persians, whatever is signed into law by the king cannot be changed.

When Daniel heard about this, he went home, opened the window toward Jerusalem, and continued his practice of praying three times a day, just as he had done before. The two vice regents and the local governors knew Daniel's routine, so they watched to see if Daniel would break the king's law or not. When he did, they went to the king and said, "Your Majesty, didn't you make a decree restricting petitions to anyone, god or man, except you, for 30 days?"

Darius said, "Yes, I did. And it cannot be changed."

Then they told him that Daniel was continuing to pray three times a day. They reminded the king that Daniel was a captive from Judah and that all he seemed to think about was Jerusalem. He should be thrown into the lions' den.

When Darius heard that, he was sorry he had signed that law and did his best to find a way to release Daniel. He tried all day, but there was no way around it.

Toward evening the men came back and insisted that the law be carried out. Reluctantly Darius gave his permission, and Daniel was arrested and taken to the lions' den. Before he was thrown in, the king said to Daniel, "May the God you love and serve deliver you!"

Then they threw Daniel into the lions' den and rolled a stone over its mouth. The king, the vice regents, and the governors sealed it with their seals. The king returned to his palace, but he was not happy with himself. That night he couldn't sleep and refused to eat, drink, or be entertained, thinking about Daniel.

First thing in the morning he returned to the lions' den and called down, "Daniel, was your God able to deliver you?"

Daniel called back, "Your Majesty! May you live forever! My God has sent His angel to shut the lions' mouths so they wouldn't hurt me. He knows that I am innocent and have done nothing against the king."

The king was overjoyed and ordered the stone rolled away and Daniel pulled up out of the den. This was done, and when he was examined, not one scratch was found on his body!

Then Darius ordered that the men involved in the plot be arrested and thrown into the lions' den, together with their wives and children. In a matter of minutes the lions overpowered them, crushed their bones, and had a feast.

Next the king issued this decree: "Peace to all of you. I am making a law for the whole kingdom that everyone shall respect the God of Daniel. He is the living God, and His kingdom will never end. He saves and rescues whomever He will and works miracles in heaven and on earth that no other god can. He is the one who delivered Daniel from the lions' den."

Daniel was reinstated to his former position and continued to serve Darius and then Cyrus, kings of Medo-Persia (Dan. 6).

Prophecy 4

Daniel's Visions

Four Beasts

It was in the first year of the reign of Belshazzar, king of Babylon, that Daniel had a vision with several scenes that he recorded:

This first vision I had was during the night. I saw the ocean being whipped up by powerful winds coming from all directions. Then I saw four huge animals come up out of the ocean, one after another, and then disappear.

The first one was a powerful lion with the wings of an eagle. The wings were then torn off, and it stood up on two legs like a man. It was given the heart and mind of a man and stopped acting like a lion.

The second animal was a huge bear with powerful jaws and paws. It had three ribs in its mouth, and one shoulder was higher than the other. A voice told it to eat as much meat as it wanted.

The third animal was a tremendous leopard with four heads and four wings. It was very powerful, and nothing could stand in its way.

The fourth animal was hard to describe. It was huge and looked hideous. It was terrifying, with large iron teeth, which it used to crush and eat everything it killed. It had 10 horns on its head, and as I focused on the horns, I saw a little horn come up. It pushed three of the other horns out of the way and took their place. This new horn had human eyes and a mouth that boasted great things.

Before this fourth animal disappeared, the scene changed, and I had a vision of heaven. Thrones were being put in place for a special occasion. Then the Ancient of Days came and took His seat. His robe was as white as snow, and His hair was as white as wool. His throne had wheels of fire and was surrounded by flames shooting in all directions. Thousands upon thousands ministered to Him, and millions stood ready to serve Him. The court was called to order, and the record books were brought in.

While the judgment was going on, I could hear the new horn of the fourth animal boasting of its accomplishments and power. And even though the other animals had disappeared, their spirit was prolonged in the fourth animal. Finally it was killed and its body consumed in the flames.

Then the scene changed again, and I saw a man who looked like the Son of God come in a cloudy chariot to the Ancient of Days. He gave Him a glorious kingdom of people from all nations and languages that will never be destroyed or pass away.

I was really troubled by what I saw. While still in vision, I asked one of the commanding angels standing by the throne what all this meant. He said to me, "The four animals represent four kingdoms. But at the end of time, God's people will make up a kingdom that will last forever."

Then I asked him about the horn with the kindly human eyes and boasting mouth that pushed three other horns out of the way. This same horn persecuted God's people until judgment was rendered against it in the heavenly court and the people were exonerated and given the kingdom.

The angel said, "The fourth animal is the fourth kingdom, and the 10 horns are 10 kings that will take over and divide the kingdom among themselves. Then a little horn will come up and push three of them out of the way to make room for itself. It will appear to be kind and will claim to have the authority of God. It will persecute God's people and will think it has been given power to change God's law. God's people will be given into its hands for some time. Then the heavenly court will be called into session. It will take away the horn's power and destroy the fourth animal. The kingdoms of the earth will become one kingdom and will be given to God's people. That kingdom will stand forever. God Himself will be their king, and everyone there will serve and obey Him."

This ended the conversation. Though I was still troubled by what I had seen and heard. But I kept it all to myself (Dan. 7).

VISIONS AND DREAMS

A Ram and a Goat

In the third year of the reign of Belshazzar, king of Babylon, I had another vision. I was on business for the king in the city of Shushan. One day I was walking along the bank of the Ulai River, and as I looked out at the water, I was given a vision.

I saw a huge ram standing on the opposite bank of the river. It had two horns, one higher than the other. Then I saw it push its way north and south, and nothing could stand in its way.

Suddenly a male goat appeared, coming in from the west. It ran so fast it hardly seemed to touch the ground. It had a large pointed horn jutting out from its forehead. It charged the ram with such fury that it broke off its two horns, knocked it to the ground, and stomped on it. The goat grew bigger and stronger, but at the height of its power and strength its large horn broke off, and four smaller horns came up in its place.

One of these smaller horns sprouted a little horn, which grew larger and larger, pointing south, then east, and finally toward the Holy Land. It exalted itself against heaven, threw God's people down, and trampled on them. It even stood up against the Prince of heaven, stopped the Temple sacrifices, and threw the truth about the heavenly sanctuary to the ground, trampling it. It did all this and prospered.

Then I heard one angel ask the other angel, "How long will this go on?"

The other angel answered, "For 2,300 days. Then the truth of the heavenly sanctuary will be restored."

But I wanted to understand more of what the vision meant. Then the angel on the other side of the river said to the angel nearby, "Gabriel, help Daniel understand the vision." When I heard that, I knew that the angel I saw was the Son of God.

So Gabriel came over to where I was, and when he did, I was afraid. I fell on my knees and bowed to the ground. He said to me, "Daniel, you don't need to be afraid. You don't have to understand everything about the vision. All you need to know is that the vision of days means years and extends to the time of the end." All this took place while I was still in vision.

Then Gabriel touched me, stood me up, and continued, "Let me tell you what will happen in the future. The ram and the goat you saw represent two kingdoms. But God is still in control. The two horns of the ram represent the joint kingdoms of the Medes and Persians. The goat represents the kingdom of Greece. Its pointed horn represents its first king. But he will die, and four of his generals will divide the kingdom.

"After this, a bold little king will come from one of the little kingdoms. His influence will grow stronger and stronger and will control many nations who fight for him. He'll be crafty and will exalt himself. He'll even stand up against the Prince of heaven. He will persecute God's people and prosper. Eventually he will be destroyed, but not by human hands.

"The vision of the 2,300 days is true. But you don't need to understand more than that, because this part of the vision applies to the time of the end."

Then the vision ended, and I felt sick. I went about the king's business, but I kept thinking about the vision and wanted to know more (Dan. 8).

Daniel Prays, and Gabriel Explains

Daniel continued to pray and study until the first year of the reign of Darius the Mede, when Gabriel came and explained more of the vision. Daniel understood from what Jeremiah the prophet had written that the Jews were to be in captivity for 70 years and then would be allowed to go home.

So he fasted and prayed, "O Lord, You are a great and awesome God. You keep Your promises and have mercy on those who love You and keep Your commandments. We have sinned and done wickedly. We have rebelled and turned against the prophets who spoke in Your name to our kings and leaders and to us, Your people.

"Lord, You always do what is right, but we have disgraced You. You let us be taken captive and be scattered throughout many lands to our shame. All of us have sinned—our kings, officials, judges, and local leaders. But You are gracious, always ready to forgive. We have sinned against You, even though we are Your people. We have not listened to Your prophets and have refused to do what they said. So you brought on us what Moses said would happen. You punished Jerusalem for what we did. Even now we have not turned to You with fasting and prayer, confessing our sins, and asking for forgiveness and help to turn from our sins.

"Years ago You showed us Your power by bringing us out of Egypt. Your power is still the same. Take us out of captivity and bring us home. Don't continue to punish Jerusalem by letting it lie in ruins. People everywhere point to Jerusalem and make fun of us.

"O God, please listen to my prayer. People know that Jerusalem is Your city and that Your Temple is in ruins. For the sake of Your good name, if for no other reason, restore Jerusalem and rebuild Your Temple. We plead with You, not because we're good, but because You are.

"Please don't delay taking us back home. Through the prophet Jeremiah You promised that our captivity would be 70 years. But now Gabriel tells me about 2300 days. Does this mean You're extending that time. For Your sake and for the sake of Jerusalem, please don't do that."

As I was praying and confessing my sins and the sins of my people and pleading for Jerusalem, Gabriel came to help me. It was about the time for the evening sacrifice and my prayers.

He said to me, "Daniel, I have come to help you understand more of the vision. As soon as you began to pray, God asked me to come to explain the time mentioned in the vision that you're so concerned about. So I flew as quickly as I could to tell you that God loves you very much and to help you understand things more clearly. Listen carefully to what I have to say.

"The 70 weeks, or 490 days, you heard about in vision—each day representing a year—have nothing to do with the 70 years of your captivity. These are years of probation for your people after they return home. They are expected to turn more fully to God, to repent of their sins, and to accept His gift of righteousness.

"When the last of these 70 weeks begins, the Messiah will come to fulfill God's promise. At the close of that week He will return to God and begin His high-priestly ministry in the heavenly sanctuary. The 70 weeks, or 490 years, will begin when the Persian king issues a decree to restore and rebuild Jerusalem. The city will be rebuilt in troublous times, in spite of heavy opposition.

"In the middle of that last week they will turn the Messiah over to strangers to be put to death, but not because of anything that He has done. This will bring the ancient sacrifices to an end. During the last half of that week God will extend one last call to your people to accept His offer of righteousness, but the rulers will reject it. This will bring about the desolation of Jerusalem by foreign armies, but the nation that does this will be destroyed" (Dan. 9).

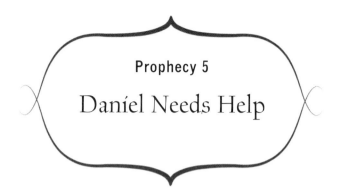

Prophecy 5

Daniel Needs Help

When Cyrus the Persian had consolidated the kingdom, he took over from his uncle Darius. In the third year of Cyrus's reign I fasted and prayed for three weeks to know the meaning of the rest of the long years mentioned in the previous visions.

Then, on the twenty-fourth day of the first month, as I was walking along the Tigris River, I looked out over the water, and suddenly I was in vision. I saw a man standing in the distance, dressed in a white linen robe with a golden belt around his waist. His whole body radiated light, his face had the appearance of lightning, his eyes flickered like flames of fire, and his arms and legs looked like the color of polished bronze. When he spoke, his voice sounded like a choir of voices. Then I knew it was the Son of God.

None of the other men with me saw this, but they knew that something strange was happening, and they were terrified. They ran. So I stood there alone and couldn't move. All my strength was gone. I slumped to the ground, totally helpless. I could hear what He was saying, but was totally unaware of anything else going on around me. It was like being fast asleep and having a powerful dream.

Suddenly a hand touched me and helped me get up on my hands and knees. It was Gabriel. I was still shaking when he said to me, "Daniel, God greatly loves you. Stand up and let me tell you what you would like to know. Your request was heard the first day you started to fast and pray. I have come to help you understand the long time period you were so concerned about in the visions.

"The reason for the three-week delay is that Cyrus, king of Persia, refused to listen to me to carry out God's plan to restore Jerusalem. Then Michael, the Son of God and Prince of heaven, came to help me. He held in check the evil powers that were influencing the king. So now I have come to help you and tell you what will happen to your people in the days ahead. I will fill in some of the details of the previous visions."

When I heard that, I was speechless and bowed my head in grief, because the other visions about my people were not good. Then Gabriel covered his brightness in order to look more like a man. He touched my lips, and I could speak again.

I said to him, "Sir, those visions were terrible, especially the last one. It scared me to death. Just thinking about it makes me lose all my strength. I'm so weak that I feel as if I'm not even breathing. But I know you can read my mind."

He touched me again, and my full strength came back. Then he said to me, "Don't be afraid. Be at peace and stay strong."

I spoke up and said, "Sir, I now feel strong enough to concentrate and listen. Please tell me more about the time in the vision."

He answered, "I've come just for that. But as soon as I do this, I will have to go back to work with Cyrus, the king of Persia, and then later with the king of Greece to make sure that God's plan for Jerusalem and His people will be carried out. First, let me tell you that no one is strong enough to contend with the forces of evil that control things on earth except God's Son, Michael, the Prince of heaven. Second, what is written in the Scripture about your people is true" (Dan. 10).

Gabriel Explains

"During the first year of Darius the Mede, I was sent to help him. Then Cyrus took over, and after him will come four more kings, the last one richer and stronger than the others. He will attack the king of Greece in order to expand his territory, but he will be defeated. The king of Greece will not only take over the kingdom of Medo-Persia, but will extend his conquests over huge areas, more than any other king has done. At the height of his power the young king will die, and his kingdom will be divided into four parts.

"The southern part will center in Egypt, and the northern part will center in Syria. Over time the northern kingdom will greatly expand, taking over Palestine and extending down to the border of Egypt. Then there will be war between the king in the south and the king in the north. Finally they will make peace and form an alliance, but the alliance will not last.

"The king in the south will attack the king in the north and will carry back to Egypt much of his riches, including his gods. After some years of peace the king in the north will retaliate and attack the king in the south, but will not be able to defeat him. The sons of the king in the north will put together a large army, but the king in the south will defeat them too. The king in the north will go back home and gather an even larger army to come against the king in the south.

"Some of your people will try to take advantage of the situation to further their own national interests and carry out God's plan for Jerusalem, but it will not work. Then the king in the north will sweep into Palestine, and the king in the south will not be able to stand up against him. The king in the north will try to force your people to adopt the religion and culture of the Greeks, but he will not succeed.

"Later the king in the north will take over the territory of Greece and Syria and push into Palestine, even casting his shadow over Egypt. The king in the south will give him his daughter in marriage, but she will not stand by his side. So he will turn his attention to the coastlands in the north, defeat those people, and return home victorious. But his arrogance and pride will be his downfall. He will be assassinated by one of his own friends. He will be followed by a king who will issue a decree that people in all territories should be taxed to help support the empire.

"He will die peacefully, not in battle. The next king will seize the throne by political intrigue, and no one will dare oppose him. He will have a huge army and will grow stronger and stronger. It will be during his reign that the Prince of the Covenant will be killed.

"His armies will continue to be successful, but his worst enemies will be those who eat from his own table. Each general will have his own army, and they will fight among themselves. Two kings will sit at the same table, lying to each other. At God's appointed time both will come to their end. Another king will set his heart on Jerusalem, take the city, and destroy it. He will return with great riches" (Dan. 11:1-28).

A New King

Gabriel continued, "Then another king will rule the empire. He will try to restore its glory, but barbarian hordes as fearless as the sailors of Cyprus will attack. To hold the eastern and western parts of the empire together, he will support those who turn against God's covenant and claim authority over what is happening in the heavenly sanctuary.

"This will produce a new power and a new king of the north. He will seduce those who oppose him with smooth and slippery talk and will lie to God's people. But those who really love God will resist him, and for this they will be tortured and killed. This will go on for some time. Many will die, but many more will be added.

"The king of this new power will exalt himself above other rulers and will claim to speak for God. He will sit in his temple and speak as if he were God. He will form an alliance with other powers to accomplish his objectives. He will honor the god of power and wealth—of gold, silver, and jewels. He will bless those who look up to him, and they will rule over cities and nations—at a price.

"He will make an alliance with a king who has many chariots, horsemen, and ships. This king will respond like a whirlwind against those who push against him. His armies will sweep through many countries like a flood, and he will extend his influence over many other nations, including the land of Egypt. Even the Promised Land will not escape. He will control the treasures of the world, and his wealth will exceed the nations of the ancient world.

"News from the east and the north will alarm him, and he will lash out with great fury to protect his kingdom. The land between the sea and the glorious holy mountain will come under his control, but he will come to his end, and no one will help him" (Dan. 11:29-45).

The Time of the End

Gabriel concluded, "During the time of the end, Michael, the Prince of heaven, who stands watch over His people, will finish His work in heaven and bring things to a close on earth.

"There will be a time of trouble such as never was before. But God's people will be delivered—everyone whose name is written in His book. Many who sleep in the grave will be resurrected and given eternal life. They will shine as bright as the stars of heaven. Others will be resurrected to their shame and destruction.

"For now, you need to stop writing, roll up your scroll, and seal it. When the time of the end comes, many will read what you have written. People will be busy traveling everywhere, and knowledge will increase."

Then the scene changed, and I saw two beings standing by the Tigris River. One was the Son of God, dressed in white linen, and the other was Gabriel, who had helped me understand the prophecies. I heard Gabriel ask the Son of God how long all this would take.

He answered, "It will take some time." I knew this meant many years.

I asked Gabriel, "Sir, what will happen after those years?"

He answered, "At that time many people will purify their lives and take their stand for God. But the wicked will refuse to change. From the time when the truth of the heavenly sanctuary was first repressed to the time of the end will be more than 1,000 years. Blessed are those who live during the years that follow. But for now, go about your work. Soon you will rest with your ancestors, but what you have written will help God's people. When the Lord returns, you will be resurrected and rewarded for what you have done" (Dan. 12).

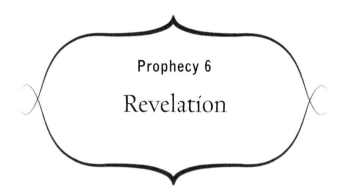

Prophecy 6

Revelation

"I, John, an apostle of Jesus Christ, am sending this message to the seven churches in Asia Minor. Grace to you and peace from God the Father, who always was, who is, and who is coming, from the Holy Spirit by God's throne, and from Jesus Christ, the Faithful One. He is the One who rose from the dead and has all the rights of a firstborn son.

"He is the rightful ruler over all kings and authorities of this world. He is the one who loved us and gave His life for us to set us free from the holding power of sin. He has made us into a kingdom of priests in the service of God the Father. To Him be glory and power for ever and ever. Amen.

"I am your brother and fellow sufferer. Even though I was arrested and sentenced to death, the Lord intervened, and I have been exiled to the prison island of Patmos. All this happened because I believed the Word of God and proclaimed the truth about Jesus Christ (Rev. 1:4-6, 9).

Revelation

"This book is about Jesus and the things God told Him to share with us concerning the future. He appeared to me and spoke to me through His angel, and I wrote down everything I saw and heard.

"Blessed are those who read this book. And blessed are those who listen to what is read and who do what it says. The time is near when all these things will begin to happen.

"The Lord will come in the clouds of heaven, and everyone will see Him, including those who killed Him. People from every nation will grieve because He's coming to carry out judgment against them. And so it will be.

"He said, 'I am the Alpha and the Omega, the Beginning and

End, the All-powerful One who always was, who is, and who is coming (Rev. 1:1-3, 7, 8).

A Vision

"I was alone worshipping on the Lord's Day, the Sabbath, when I heard behind me a loud voice like a trumpet, saying, 'I also am the Beginning and the End. Write what you will see and hear in a little book and send it to the congregations in Ephesus, Smyrna, Pergamos, Thyatira, Sardis, Philadelphia, and Laodicea.'

"I turned to see who had spoken to me, and I saw seven golden lampstands, and the Son of God was walking among them. He wore the same daily dress that the high priest wore when he ministered in the sanctuary—a long, white robe and a golden belt. His hair was white as snow, and His eyes looked as if they were on fire. His feet looked like polished brass, and His voice sounded like the roar of a waterfall. He had seven stars in His right hand. When He spoke, a laser sword flashed from His mouth. His face was as bright as the noonday sun.

"I closed my eyes and fell at His feet, as lifeless as if I were dead. He touched me with His right hand and said, 'Don't be afraid. I am the First and the Last. I am the one who was dead and is alive. I will never die again, but will live for ever. I have the keys to the prison house of death and the grave.

"'Get up and write what you saw and what I will show you. Some things apply to both the present and the future. The seven stars you saw in My right hand represent the leaders of the seven churches, and the golden lampstands are the seven congregations'" (Rev. 1:10-20).

History of the Christian Church
Letter to Ephesus

"From John to the leader of the church in Ephesus:

"This message is from the One who walks among the churches. He says, 'I know all about you. I know your commitment, how hard you work for Me, and that you can't tolerate duplicity and evil. You have tested those who claim to be apostles and found them to be frauds and liars. You are to be commended for your perseverance and loyalty to what's right.

"'But I need to point out something to you. You have lost the first love you had for Me. So turn around and go back to when you first met Me. Be motivated by that love, or I'll have to take away your lampstand. Yet there is a lot of good about you. You hate how the Nicolaitans twist the gospel and undermine your faith, which I hate too.

"'You have ears, so listen to what the Holy Spirit is telling you. Whoever holds on to Me I will give the right to eat fruit from the tree of life which is in the middle of the Garden of God' (Rev. 2:1-7).

Letter to Smyrna

"From John to the leader of the church in Smyrna.

"This message is from the One who is the First and the Last, who was dead and is alive. He says, 'I know your troubles and distress. I know your sufferings and poverty. But you are rich because of your faith and love for Me. I know how those who claim to be My people slander and accuse you of evil. They're doing exactly what Satan wants them to do.

"'Don't be afraid of what's coming. Some of you will be arrested and thrown into prison. Your faith will be severely tested. This persecution will last for some time. Be faithful to Me, even if it means you have to die. I will resurrect you and give you the crown of life.

"'You have ears, so listen to what the Holy Spirit is telling you. Those who die for Me now will not have to die the second death' (Rev. 2:8-11).

Letter to Pergamos

"From John to the leader of the church in Pergamos:

"This letter is from the One who has a laser sword in His mouth. He says, 'I know where you live. I know that Satan has set up his temporary headquarters there. But you continued to hold on to Me, even after you saw Antipas arrested and killed for refusing to worship Caesar.

"'Yet I need to point out something to you. Some among you act like Balaam. He got the people of Israel to compromise their faith by luring them into adultery and idol worship. And you— you're listening to the Nicolaitans, who are twisting the gospel and undermining your faith. You need to repent and change or I'll have to use the sword in My mouth and take action against your church.

"'You have ears, so listen to what the Holy Spirit is telling you. Everyone who is loyal to Me will eat the manna of heaven and will be given a new name engraved on a white stone' (Rev. 2:12-17).

Letter to Thyatira

"From John to the leader of the church in Thyatir:.

"This message is from the One whose eyes look like they're on fire and whose feet look like polished brass. He says, 'I know your faith and love, your perseverance and good deeds, and that you're doing more for Me now than ever before.

"'But I need to point out something to you. You have let false doctrines come in among you, like those Jezebel brought in to Israel. She called herself a prophetess. She encouraged actual adultery as part of idol worship. I gave her time to repent, but she didn't.

"'Those who worship idols will suffer terribly unless they repent. And those who follow her teachings will be killed as she was. Then the church will know that I search hearts and minds and reward each one according to what he has done.

"'But for those of you in Thyatira who have not listened to Satan, all I ask of you is to hold on to your faith. When I come, I will share My power and authority with those who have been faithful, and they will help decide the fate of nations. This is according to My Father's will. As the Scripture says, "The Lord will sit in judgment on the nations and break their power as easily as if it were a clay jar."

"'You have ears, so listen to what the Holy Spirit is telling you. When sin is no more, you will shine as the morning star' (Rev. 2:18-29).

Letter to Sardis

"From John to the leader of the church in Sardis:

"This message is from the One who, through the Holy Spirit, holds the seven stars in His hand. He says, 'I know what you're doing. You have a good reputation, and it looks to others like you're all for Me when you're not. Wake up! Strengthen the love for Me you do have so that it doesn't die. God is not pleased with what you're doing.

"'Remember what you were taught and do it. If you don't wake up and change, I'll have to take control. You won't know when I will do this, but it will be as unexpected as a thief in the night.

"'A few in Sardis have not soiled their clothes. They will walk beside Me in white because they're worthy. All who overcome will be dressed in white, and I will not take their names out of the Book of Life but will acknowledge them as Mine before the Father and the angels.

"'You have ears, so listen to what the Holy Spirit is telling you' (Rev. 3:1-6).

Letter to Philadelphia

"From John to the leader of the church in Philadelphi:.

"This message is from the Holy One, the one who is true, who has the keys of the kingdom of David to open and lock doors, which no one else can do. He says, 'I know what your good deeds are and that you love Me. I have opened a door for you, but you don't have enough strength to go through it on your own. Yet you have kept My word and not turned away from Me.

"'Those from the synagogue of Satan who listen to his suggestions are not real Jews, no matter what they say. I will stop them from speaking against you and will make them see that I love you.

"'Because you have kept my Word and remained faithful, I will be with you during the testing time that will come upon the whole world. I am coming soon, so hold on and don't let anyone take away your faith and cause you to end up losing your crown of life.

"'Those who are faithful will be pillars in the temple of My God. You will never have to leave. I will write My name on you, along with the name of My God and the name of His city, the New Jerusalem, which will come down from heaven.

"'You have ears, so listen to what the Holy Spirit is telling you' (Rev. 3:7-13).

Letter to Laodicea

"From John to the leader of the church in Laodicea:

"This message is from the 'Amen,' the Faithful and True Witness, who created all things under the direction of God. He says, 'I know the good things you do, but you're neither cold nor hot toward Me. I wish you were one way or the other so that people could tell where you stand. You taste like stagnant water because you keep talking about how spiritually rich you are and how much money you have. You think you don't need anything. But you don't realize that you are spiritually poor, blind, and naked. You are to be pitied.

"'I urge you to buy the gold I'm offering you, which has been refined in the fire. That is what will make you rich. I'm also offering you a white robe to cover your nakedness so that you won't have to be ashamed. And I have ointment for your eyes, to help you see things as you should.

"'I discipline those I love because I care about them. So be in earnest and change your attitude. I'm knocking at your heart's door. When you hear Me calling, come and open the door. I'll be happy to come in, and we can eat together.

"'Don't give in to the world, and I will give you a place to sit with Me on my throne, just as I didn't give in to the world and am sitting next to My Father on His throne.

"'You have ears, so listen to what the Holy Spirit is telling you' (Rev. 3:14–22).

The Throne Room

"After I got the letters off, I had another vision. I saw an open door in heaven. And I heard a voice that sounded like a trumpet, calling, 'Come on up! I will then show you things that will happen in the future.'

"The Holy Spirit took hold of me, and the next thing I knew, I was in heaven. There was an open door, and I saw a throne and Someone sitting on it. I knew it must be God. A light sparkling like diamonds covered God's face, and a rainbow was above the throne.

"In a semicircle in front of the throne were 24 smaller thrones, and on them sat 24 elders dressed in white with golden crowns on their heads. Lightning flashed around God's throne, and there were sounds of thunder and the roar of a coming storm. Seven burning torches were in front of the throne, representing the Holy Spirit. There also was an open courtyard before the throne that looked like a large sea. It was as clear as crystal and as smooth as glass.

"There were four angel guards standing near the four corners of the throne. The first represented the power of a lion, the next the service of an ox, the third the intelligence of man, and the fourth the speed of an eagle. They were dressed in robes which were covered with eyes from front to back. Each one had six wings, and they never slept day or night. They were singing, 'Holy, holy, holy is the Lord God Almighty, the one who always was, who is, and who will come!'

"When the four angels gave glory and honor and thanks to God, the 24 elders laid their crowns in front of Him, fell on their knees, and worshipped the One who lives for ever and ever, saying, 'You are worthy, O Lord our God, to receive glory and honor and to exercise Your power, because You created all things and by Your will they continue to exist' (Rev. 4).

The Lamb

"The One who sat on the throne had a scroll in His hand. It was written on both sides, front and back, and sealed in seven sections.

"A powerful angel called out: 'Who is qualified to break the seals and open the scroll?' No one was. When I saw that no one could, I cried. One of the elders said to me, 'Don't cry. The Lion from the house of David out of the tribe of Judah is qualified. He will break the seals and open the scroll.'

"Then I saw a Lamb standing in the middle of the elders, facing the throne and the four angel guards. It looked as if it had been killed. It had seven eyes and seven little horns which represented His wisdom and power, working through the Holy Spirit all over the world.

"The Lamb was the Son of God. As High Priest He stepped forward and took the scroll out of the hand of the One who sat on the throne. When He did, the four angels and the 24 elders fell on their knees, bowed before the Lamb, and worshipped Him.

"As they stood, I saw that each elder had a harp and a golden bowl holding the incense of the prayers of God's people, and together they sang, 'You are worthy to take the scroll and break the seals, because You gave Your life for us and bought our redemption by Your own blood. You took us from different tribes and nations and made us kings and priests, to serve God and to rule with Him on the earth made new.'

"Then I heard the voices of many angels join the four mighty ones and the elders, singing, 'Worthy is the Lamb that was sacrificed to receive power and riches, wisdom and strength, and honor, glory, and praise!'

"Voices from all over heaven and earth, and voices from the sea joined in singing: 'To the One who sits on the throne and to the Lamb be praise, honor, glory, and power for ever and ever!'

"The four angels shouted, 'Amen!' and the 24 elders fell on their knees and worshipped God and the Lamb" (Rev. 5).

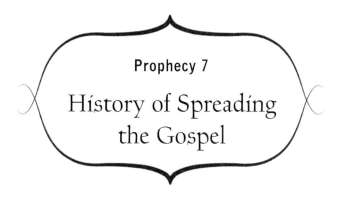

Prophecy 7

History of Spreading the Gospel

The First Seal

"When the Lamb broke the first seal and unrolled that section of the scroll, the first angel guard said, 'Come! See what's happening!'

"I looked and saw a white horse, and the One who sat on it had a bow in His hand and arrows strapped to His back. I saw a crown of victory placed on His head, and He rode across the earth, spreading the gospel for God (Rev. 6:1, 2).

The Second Seal

"When the Lamb broke the second seal and unrolled that section of the scroll, the second angel said, 'Come! See what's happening!'

"I looked and saw another horse. This one was red, and the one who sat on it had a huge sword in his hand and was given permission to take away peace from the earth. Then persecution came, and many of God's people were killed (Rev. 6:3, 4).

The Third Seal

"When the Lamb broke the third seal and unrolled the next section of the scroll, the third angel said, 'Come! See what's happening!'

"I looked and saw a black horse. The one who sat on it had a scale in his hand. Then I heard a voice coming from among the four powerful angels, saying, 'Food will be scarce. It will cost a day's wages just to buy a quart of wheat or three quarts of barley. But this will not hurt the spiritual oil and wine' (Rev. 6:5, 6).

The Fourth Seal

"Then the Lamb broke the fourth seal and unrolled that section of the scroll. When He did, the fourth angel said, 'Come! See what's happening!'

"I looked and saw a pale horse, and the one who sat on it was called 'Death.' Wherever he rode his horse, graves popped up in his tracks. He swung his sword and brought violence, hunger, disease, and death to one fourth of the earth (Rev. 6:7, 8).

The Fifth Seal

"Next the Lamb broke the fifth seal and unrolled that section of the scroll. I looked and saw an altar, and next to it lay the bodies of those who had been killed because they were true to the Word of God and held to their testimony.

"Their bodies cried out, 'How much longer, Lord? You are holy and true. How much longer before You come and judge those who shed our blood?'

"Then white robes were given to them, and they were told to wait a little longer until the death decree against their brothers and sisters was stopped (Rev. 6:9-11).

The Sixth Seal

"When the Lamb broke the sixth seal and unrolled this section of the scroll, there was a huge earthquake. The sun turned dark, and the moon turned red. The sky was full of falling stars, dropping like figs from a tree blown by a strong wind.

"After that the sky rolled back like a scroll, and every mountain and island was moved out of place. The kings of the earth, the generals, the rich and powerful of the earth, and every free man and slave fled to the mountains to hide in caves or among the rocks, saying, 'Cover us and hide us from the face of the One sitting on the throne and from the Lamb! The day of judgment has come! Who can survive?' (Rev. 6:12-17).

The Sealing

"Then I saw four angels assigned to hold back the winds of judgment from blowing across the land or destroying the trees of the Lord. A fifth angel came from the east with the seal of God in his hand. He called out to the four angels, 'Don't let go of the winds until we have sealed God's people for eternity.'

"I heard the number of those who were sealed—12,000 from each of the tribes of spiritual Israel, a total of 144,000. Then I saw a sea of people too large to count, from every nation, tribe, and language, standing before the throne in white robes with palm branches in their hands. They broke out in songs of praise, singing, 'Salvation comes from our God, the one who sits on the throne, and from the Lamb!'

"Then the angels formed a circle around the throne, the four guards, and the 24 elders. They fell on their knees and bowed to the ground in worship. Then they stood up and sang: 'Praise and glory, wisdom and thanksgiving, honor and power to our God for ever and ever. Amen!'

"One of the elders asked me, 'Who are these people in white robes? Where did they come from?'

"I answered, 'I don't know, but I'm sure you do.'

"He said, 'These are the ones who have washed themselves in the blood of the Lamb and have gone through the troubles of the last days. That's why you see them standing before the throne. God has given them a special place of honor. He will be among them, and they will serve Him continuously.

"'They will never go hungry or thirst again, nor will they have to suffer the scorching heat of the sun. The Lamb will be their shepherd and will lead them to springs of living water. And God Himself will wipe away all tears from their eyes' (Rev. 7).

The Seventh Seal

"Then I saw the Lamb break the seventh seal and unroll the last section of the scroll. When He did, there was a silence of anticipation in heaven awaiting the arrival of the saints (Rev. 8:1).

History of Wars
Seven Trumpets

"Next I saw seven angels come up to the throne, and God gave each one a trumpet. I saw a small golden altar before God's throne and another angel with a censer standing there. He was given large amounts of incense, which represented the prayers of God's people.

He offered them on the altar, and the smoke of the incense rose up in front of the throne.

"Then the angel filled his censer with fire from the little golden altar and threw the censer down to earth. There were flashes of lightning, peals of thunder, and a powerful earthquake. This alerted the seven angels, and they got ready to blow their trumpets (Rev. 8:2-6).

The First Trumpet

"The first angel blew his trumpet, and fire and hail the color of blood came down on the earth. One third of the trees and all the green grass were burned up (Rev. 8:7).

The Second Trumpet

"Then the second angel blew his trumpet, and an erupting volcano, together with the whole mountain, was thrown into the sea, and one third of the ocean turned to blood. A third of the fish died, and many ships were destroyed (Rev. 8:8, 9).

The Third Trumpet

"Next the third angel blew his trumpet, and a huge burning meteor fell from heaven. It hit a third of the earth's rivers and sources of water. The name of the meteor was 'Bitterness,' because a third of the waters turned bitter and people died from drinking it (Rev. 8:10, 11).

The Fourth Trumpet

"When the fourth angel blew his trumpet, the sun, moon, and stars lost one third of their brightness. There was no light for one third of the day and one third of the night. An angel flying overhead cried out, 'Woe! Woe! Woe! Terrible times are coming when the next three angels blow their trumpets' (Rev. 8:12, 13).

The Fifth Trumpet

"Then the fifth angel blew his trumpet, and this brought on the first terrible woe. I saw an angel come down from heaven with a key to the demonic pit. When he opened the pit, smoke shot up as if coming out of a huge furnace. The smoke was so thick that it blocked the rays of the sun and poisoned the air.

"Out of the smoke came an army of locusts. They were told not to harm any growing grass or green tree or plant, but only those who did not have the seal of God. They were given power to sting but not to kill. This lasted for some time. People wanted to die rather than live.

"These locusts were huge—more like horses ready for war. On their backs were strange-looking riders who had something like crowns on their heads, and their long hair looked like women's hair. Each rider had an iron breastplate, and when they gave the battle cry, they looked as vicious as attacking lions.

"They rode into battle as if they had wings, and the thunder of their horses' hooves sounded like thousands of chariot wheels. The horses had tails like scorpion stingers with which to hurt people. This went on for some time. The king over them was in charge of the demonic pit. His name in both Hebrew and Greek means 'Destroyer.'

"The first woe is past, but two more are coming (Rev. 9:1-12).

The Sixth Trumpet

"After this, the sixth angel blew his trumpet, and the second woe began. I heard a voice coming from the direction of the little golden altar before the throne of God, saying to the sixth angel, 'Tell the four angels holding back the river Euphrates to let go.'

"The four angels let go, and the river overflowed for some time, killing a third of the people. The number of mounted troops who attacked the people over days, months, and years numbered in the millions. Their breastplates glistened in the sun, making them look like they were on fire. A third of the people were killed by the fire, smoke, and fumes that came out of the horses' mouths.

"The people who survived did not turn to God for help, but continued worshipping idols of gold, silver, bronze, stone, or wood, which cannot see or hear. They did not repent, but continued their murders, witchcraft, immorality, and stealing (Rev. 9:13-21).

The Little Scroll

"During this time the Son of God came down from heaven in

the form of a powerful angel. He was wrapped in a cloud and had a rainbow over His head. His face was as bright as the sun, and His legs looked like pillars of fire. He was holding a little scroll in His hand.

"He set His right foot on the sea and His left foot on the land. He called out in a loud voice that sounded like the roar of a lion. Then I heard seven voices as loud as thunder respond with frightening words. I was ready to write down what I heard, but a voice said to me, 'Don't write it down, because for now these words are sealed.'

"Then the Son of God raised His hand to heaven and, in the name of God who created heaven and earth, took a vow that there would be no long delay, but that during the sounding of the seventh trumpet, the spreading of the gospel would be finished as the prophets had predicted.

"The voice that told me not to write also said to me, 'Go up to the Son of God, and take the little scroll and eat it.' So I went up and asked Him to let me have the little scroll. He gave it to me and said, 'Take it and eat it. It will taste sweet in your mouth, but it will give you a sour stomach.' So I took the little scroll and ate it. In my mouth it tasted sweet, but it gave me a sour stomach, just as He had said.

"Then I was told that God's message must yet be taken to many nations, people, languages, and kings (Rev. 10).

The Word of God

"After that I was given a measuring rod and told to measure God's temple, the altar, and those who worship Him. I was told not to measure the outer courtyard, because those who were there have been trampling down holy things and will do so for some time.

"The two testaments of God's Word were like two witnesses. They had power to speak during that time and did so with grief in their hearts. They received their oil from the two olive trees and their light from the two lamps that stood in the presence of God.

"If anyone tried to hurt the two witnesses, they had been given the power of Elijah to call fire down from heaven on God's enemies and to close up the sky so it wouldn't rain. They also had power to turn water into blood and to bring on plagues, as Moses did in Egypt.

"The leader from the demonic pit went to war against the two witnesses, trying to silence them. It looked as if he had succeeded, because the people saw the two witnesses lying dead in the streets of the city—a city as sinful as Sodom and as rebellious as Egypt. People continued crucifying the Lord in their hearts.

"This lasted for some time, and people thought it was the end of the two testaments. They celebrated because they didn't have to listen to the witnesses anymore or be disturbed by their prophecies. But the Holy Spirit breathed life into the two witnesses, and they stood to their feet. When the people saw this, they became frightened. I heard a voice say to the two witnesses, 'Come up here!' As their enemies watched, they went up in a cloud and stood in the sky.

"Then a great earthquake shook the city, and one-tenth of it was destroyed. Thousands of people were killed, and the rest were afraid and honored God as they had never done before.

"The second woe has passed, and the third woe is coming (Rev. 11:1-14).

The Seventh Trumpet

"Then the seventh angel blew his trumpet, and there were voices in heaven, saying, 'The kingdoms of this world were given by God to His Son, and He will reign for ever and ever.'

"The 24 elders I had seen earlier fell on their knees, bowed to the ground, and worshipped the One on the throne. They said, 'We thank You, Lord. You are the Mighty One, the One who was, who is, and ever will be. You have taken Your great power and have begun to rule.

"'The nations of the world have turned against You. The time of Your judgment has come, the time to judge the living and the dead. You will reward all those who have served You and honored Your name, whether they were small or great. And You will destroy those who exploited the earth.'

"Another door opened into the temple of God in heaven, and I saw the ark of the covenant containing the law of God. Then there were flashes of lightning, peals of thunder, a global earthquake, and a tremendous hailstorm. The third woe ended, and so did the history of the world" (Rev. 11:15-19).

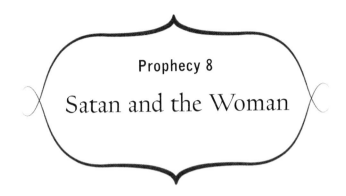

Prophecy 8
Satan and the Woman

John continued:

"In vision I saw a woman in the sky. She was standing on the moon, dressed with the light of the sun, with a crown of 12 stars on her head. She was pregnant and cried out in pain, ready to give birth.

"Then I saw something else in the sky. It was a huge red dragon. It had seven heads with seven crowns and 10 horns. With its long tail it swept a third of the stars out of the sky and threw them down to earth. It had its eyes on the woman, ready to kill her baby soon after He was born. But her Son was destined to rule all nations. So God took Him to heaven to sit next to Him on His throne.

"Then the woman had to flee into the wilderness to survive. God guided her to a place where she would be taken care of for some time to come (Rev. 12:1-6).

War in Heaven

"Next I had a vision of eternity past and the war in heaven. The huge red dragon, called 'the devil' and 'Satan,' had rejected the authority of the Son of God, who is known as 'Michael.' So Michael and His angels had to fight against the dragon and his angels. The huge dragon, that ancient serpent was defeated and thrown out of heaven, and his angels with him.

"Then I heard a voice from heaven, saying, 'Heaven is now safe. The kingdom of God is secure, and the authority of Christ is no longer challenged. The devil, who falsely accused God's Son, is now accusing the followers of Christ day and night. But they are overcoming him by the power of the blood of the Lamb and by the Word of God, and they are not afraid to die.

" 'Let heaven rejoice! But this is not the end of things. The devil is angry with those on earth because he knows his time is short' (Rev. 12:7-12).

The War Continues

"When Satan realized that his activity was confined to this earth, he went after the woman. But God gave her two huge wings, which she used to fly to the place in the wilderness He had prepared for her. There she would be safe from the dragon's intent to kill her.

"Then the dragon decided to flood her out. But God opened the earth and it swallowed up the flood. This made the devil furious, and he attacked the woman's descendants who love God, keep His commandments, and by faith hold on to what Jesus said (Rev. 12:13-17).

The Final Battle

"Then I saw a terrible-looking animal come out of the sea. It had seven heads and 10 horns with crowns. On each of its seven heads was a word that insulted God.

"This huge animal had the body of a leopard, the feet of a powerful bear, and the mouth of a ferocious lion. Satan was nearby and gave this animal demonic power and great authority.

"As I looked, I saw this terrible-looking animal receive a deadly blow to one of its heads. But amazingly the wound healed. The whole world marveled at its recovery and began listening to this animal. People said to each other, 'Who can stand up against such a powerful animal and make war with it?' So they worshipped this animal and, by doing so, were worshipping the dragon who gave it its power.

"This terrible-looking animal became very proud and claimed to speak for God. It was allowed to do this and to exercise its authority for some time. What it said and did during this time was an insult to God and to all of heaven.

"It attacked God's people and was soon able to exercise its authority over every tribe, language, and nation. Everyone whose name was not written in the Lamb's book of life ended up worshipping this animal.

"If you have ears, you need to listen to what I'm telling you.

Those who take God's people captive and will kill them must be taken captive and killed. This will call for a strong faith and special endurance on the part of God's people (Rev. 13:1-10).

The Battle Intensifies

"Next I saw a huge animal come out of the earth. This one was different. It had two little horns like a young ram, but it had the voice of a dragon. It stood next to the terrible-looking animal and used its authority to force the whole world to worship the animal whose head wound had healed.

"This huge animal with two little horns did many marvelous things. It even made fire come down from heaven in front of people. These things deceived the people and made them listen to what this land animal had to say. It told them to worship the animal who had received a deadly blow yet lived. Those who refused would be killed. Everyone had to receive an identification mark on his right hand or forehead, whether small or great, rich or poor, free or slave. No one could buy or sell unless he had the worship mark with the name and number of the first animal.

"This calls for special wisdom. Those with spiritual insight will know to whom the name and number belongs. The number is 666, which stands for the power and authority of a man (Rev. 13:11-18).

The Lamb of God

"The scene changed and I saw the Lamb of God standing on Mount Zion. With Him were the 144,000 with His Father's name on their foreheads.

"Then I heard a voice from heaven that sounded like the roar of a huge waterfall or loud thunder. I heard the music of a harp and a new song being sung by those who were with the Lamb. They sang this song in front of the four mighty angels and the 24 elders. No one was able to learn and sing this song of redemption like as they could.

"The 144,000 were like the first fruits of the redeemed from all over the earth. Their faith was pure, and they followed the Lamb wherever He led them. In their mouth was no dishonesty, and they stood blameless before God as a sample of God's great harvest of all to be redeemed (Rev. 14:1-5).

VISIONS AND DREAMS

Three Angels

"Again the scene changed, and I saw an angel flying high up in the sky with a special message of the gospel for everyone on earth— for every tribe, language, and nation. He announced with a loud voice, 'Honor God and give glory to him, for the time of judgment has come. Worship the One who created heaven and earth, oceans, and springs of water.'

"Next I saw another angel flying high up in the sky. He announced to everyone on earth: 'That great spiritual city called Babylon that men have built has fallen from the truth about God and will continue to fall, because she is making all nations drink her polluted wine.'

"Then I saw a third angel flying high up in the sky, announcing with a loud voice, 'If anyone worships the first creature or the second one and has the identity mark on his forehead or his hand, he will not escape the justice of God. He will face annihilation by fire in the presence of the holy angels and in the presence of the Lamb. The smoke will rise until all is burned up. No relief or hope will be available for those who worship the two creatures and choose to receive their identifying mark.'

"What I saw calls for special endurance on the part of God's people who are committed to keeping God's commandments and are faithful to Jesus.

"Then I heard a voice from heaven say, 'Write all this down. Blessed are those who die in the Lord.' 'Yes,' says the Holy Spirit, 'they will rest from all their work, and what they did will not be forgotten'"(Rev. 14:6-13).

The Harvest

"The scene changed, and I saw a huge white cloud. On it sat Jesus, the Son of Man. He had on His head a crown of gold and in His hand a sharp sickle. An angel came out of the temple in heaven and called to Jesus, 'Now is the time to reap the earth's harvest, because it is ripe!' So Jesus swung His sickle and the harvest was reaped.

"Then another angel came out of the heavenly temple, and he too had a sharp sickle. A third angel came out of the temple with fire in his hand. He called to that angel, 'Use your sickle to cut the clusters of grapes off the vine, because the grapes are ripe for judgment!' So that's what the angel did. Then he threw the grapes into God's winepress outside the heavenly city, and blood came out. It flowed everywhere. This meant the wicked would be destroyed and be gone forever (Rev. 14:14-20).

The Song of Deliverance

"Next I saw seven angels coming out of the temple. Also, I saw what looked like a sea as smooth as glass with fire underneath. On the sea stood those who had rejected the identifying mark of the terrible creature with its name. They had harps in their hands and sang the song of Moses and the Lamb, a song of deliverance, saying:

Great and marvelous are the things the Lord our God has
   done!
He is king of nations!
His ways are right and just!
Who does not stand in awe of what He has done?
Who can refuse His greatness?
Lord, You alone are holy. All nations will bow and worship
   You because Your justice has been seen by all" (Rev. 15:1-4).

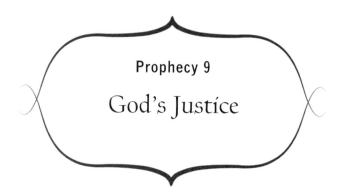

Prophecy 9

God's Justice

"Then my eyes turned back to the seven angels I had seen coming out of the heavenly temple. They were dressed in shining white robes with golden bands around their waists. One of the four angels guarding the throne gave each of the seven angels a bowl of God's justice.

"The temple was filled with smoke from His glory and power. No one could go into the temple until God's justice was carried out (Rev. 15:5-8).

Seven Angels

"Then I heard a voice calling to the seven angels, 'Go and carry out God's judgments!'

"So the first angel poured his bowl on the earth, and sores broke out on the bodies of those who had the identifying mark of the terrible-looking animal and on those who had obeyed the land animal that imitated it.

"The second angel poured his bowl on the ocean, which turned as red as blood. Every living thing in the ocean died.

"The third angel poured his bowl on the lakes and rivers and springs of water. They, too, turned as red as blood. I heard the angel say, 'Lord, You are righteous. You have always existed and always will. You have judged those who have shed the blood of Your people by turning their water red, reminding them of what they have done.' Another voice out of the temple in heaven said, 'True and right is the justice of the Lord God, the Almighty One.'

"The fourth angel poured his bowl on the sun, and its rays scorched parts of the earth and caused people to feel its intense heat. The people did not repent, but cursed God for letting this happen.

"The fifth angel poured his bowl on the palace of the sea creature that exercised such power. It became so dark that people bit their tongues in pain, but they did not repent. Like the others, they cursed God for what He had done.

"The sixth angel poured his bowl on the river Euphrates, and its water dried up. The Holy Spirit was withdrawn from the earth, and the way was opened for the battle between the King of kings and the demonic spirits, which looked like frogs coming out of the mouth of the dragon, the sea beast, and the animal who was a false prophet.

"These demonic spirits went all over the world working miracles to gather people to fight against God and His people. This is the battle of Armageddon.

"The Lord said, 'I am coming quickly. Blessed are those who stay awake and wear the garment I've given them so that they don't have to be ashamed.'

"The seventh angel poured his bowl into the air, and a loud voice from heaven declared, 'It is done!' There was lightning and thunder and an earthquake so powerful that it shook the whole world. There was never an earthquake like this before. The cities of the world crumbled, islands sank, mountains disappeared, and hailstones as huge as blocks of ice fell from the sky. The world had become as wicked as ancient Babylon. It was divided into three parts, and each part received God's judgment. The people did not turn to God, but cursed Him instead (Rev. 16).

The Woman and the Beast

"Then one of the seven angels with the seven bowls said to me, 'Come, let me show you the judgment of the prostitute who sits on the waves of the sea luring people away from God. Kings have gone to bed with her, and the people are drinking her wine.'

"The angel took me to a deserted place, and there I saw the woman sitting on a red beast that had seven heads and 10 horns. The beast had insulting words about God written all over it. The woman was beautifully dressed in red and purple and had a golden cup in her hand. She had a mysterious name on her forehead, meaning Babylon the Great, Mother of Spiritual Prostitutes, and Universal False Worship.

"The woman was drunk with the blood of God's people,

those she had killed for their faith in Jesus. When I saw this, I was stunned!

"The angel said to me, 'Why are you so shocked? Let me tell you about the mysterious working of this woman and the beast she sits on. People whose names are not in the book of life are drawn by the power of this beast which was, then was not, and now is.

"'The seven heads of the beast represent seven mountains where the woman lives. They also represent seven nations. Five have come and gone. One currently exists, and one is still to come. When it does, it will last only a short time. The dragon's kingdom is number eight, but it's really made up of the spirit of the former seven. It's like one kingdom with seven heads, and they will all be destroyed.

"'The 10 horns you saw represent 10 nations which are not yet united. For a short time they will unite and go along with the dragon. They will be of one mind and will use their power and authority to support the woman. They will fight against the Lamb of God, but the Lamb will overpower them. He is King of kings and Lord of lords, and those who stand with Him will be faithful and true.

"'The sea on which the woman and the beast sit represents people, multitudes, languages, and nations. The woman also represents the city from which the dragon controls the kings of the earth. God will let these kings go along with the woman until the time comes for Him to act. Then the nations will see that the woman has deceived them and will turn on her, strip her naked, and set her on fire' (Rev. 17).

Spiritual Babylon

"After this I saw a powerful angel with great authority come down from heaven. The whole earth was covered with light from his brightness.

"With a strong voice he called out, 'The spiritual city of Babylon has fallen! She has come under the influence of demons! Every evil spirit is there and every hateful thing. The nations are drunk with her adulterous wine, and the merchants of the earth have become rich by supplying Babylon with luxuries.'

"Then I heard another voice from heaven, saying, 'Come out of her, my people! Don't take part in her sins and have God's judgments fall on you. Her sins are piled up to heaven, and the time has come for God to act. He will treat her just as she treated you and pay her double for making you taste her harshness more than once.

"'She has lived a life of luxury and thought of herself as an eternal queen, never having to suffer, never to be a widow. But very quickly God's judgment will come and she will know sorrow, grief, and pain. She will experience famine and will be destroyed by fire. God is stsrong and powerful. He is the One who will judge her (Rev. 18:1-8).

Commercial Babylon

"'The nations will weep when they see her go up in smoke. They will watch and say, "That great and powerful city has been destroyed so quickly!"

"'The merchants will cry because their markets are gone. They had traded with her in gold and silver, sold her pearls, ivory, precious stones, linen, silk, rare woods, bronze, iron, marble, incense, spices, oils, wine, flour, wheat, cattle, sheep, horses, and wagons, and had provided her with workers.

"'All the luxuries and splendid things of Babylon are gone. And the merchants who became rich because of her are crying. They're saying, "That great city was dressed in fine linen and silk, wearing gold and precious stones and pearls. She was so wealthy, but in such a short time she has come to nothing."

"'When the ship captains and those who trade by sea and air see this, they will cry out, "There was never a city like this great city!" They will throw dust on their heads, saying, "All of us who traded with her became rich, but now she's gone!"

"'Let all of heaven rejoice and the people of God be glad. The Lord has condemned her for what she has done to His people and to those who spoke for Him.'

"Then the mighty angel picked up a huge rock and threw it into the sea, saying, 'In this same way Babylon will suddenly be thrown into the sea and disappear. Her music will end. Her musicians, flutists, harpists, drummers, and trumpeters will never be heard again. Her artists, craftsmen, farmers, and manufacturers will be gone. Her lights will be out, and in place of celebrations and the happy voices of brides and bridegrooms, there will be silence.

"'She deceived the merchants, the great men, and every nation on earth. She has blood on her hands and is responsible for killing God's people and those who spoke for Him'" (Rev. 18:9-24).

Prophecy 10

The Wedding

John continued:

"After this, the scene changed and I heard a large multitude in heaven with one voice shouting, 'Alleluia! Salvation, glory, honor, and power belong to our God! His justice is true and right! He condemned the woman who corrupted the earth with her prostitutions and killed God's people.' Again they shouted, 'Alleluia! The rebellious city is going up in smoke!'

"The 24 elders and the four mighty angels by the throne fell on their knees before God, worshipped Him, and cried out, 'Amen! Alleluia!'

"After this, a voice from the throne thundered, 'Praise God, all you who serve Him, both small and great!'

"Then the multitude in heaven spoke with a voice that sounded like the deep roar of a mighty waterfall and as loud as thunder, saying, 'Alleluia! The Lord God omnipotent reigns! Let us rejoice and be glad and give Him the glory that is due His name. The marriage of the Lamb has come! His wife is ready! She is dressed in a clean, white wedding gown given to her by the Bridegroom, embroidered with her kind deeds.'

"The mighty angel who was with me said, 'Write this down: Blessed are those who have received the invitation to the wedding and reception of the Lamb.' Then he added, 'This is what God said and His words are true.'

"I fell on my knees before the angel, but he pulled me up and said, 'Don't worship me! Worship God! I'm just one of God's servants, as you are, and as all those are who hold on to what Jesus said through the gift of prophecy' (Rev. 19:1-10).

VISIONS AND DREAMS

The King Comes

"Then I saw heaven open and the Son of God riding on a white horse, ready for war. He is faithful and true and is coming to carry out God's justice. His eyes looked as if they were on fire, and on His head was a triple crown. His robe was as red as blood. His name is the Word of God!

"The armies of heaven followed, all dressed in clean, white robes, riding white horses. His words were like a laser sword with which to fight the nations. The time for mercy and forgiveness is past. With a rod of iron He will administer the justice of Almighty God. On His robe by His thigh was written: King of kings! Lord of lords! (Rev. 19:11-16).

Enemies of the Bride Destroyed

"Next I saw a mighty angel standing in the light of the sun. He called to the vultures, 'Come! Get ready to eat the dead bodies of the leaders, the captains with their horses, and all people, small and great.'

"I saw the kings of the earth and their armies come together under the influence of the terrible creature to fight against the One on the white horse and His army. The terrible animal was captured, and so was the huge animal who deceived the people by the great things he did and by making them worship the sea animal and receive its mark.

"Both of them were thrown into a lake of fire, and the people with the identifying mark were killed by the laser sword of the One on the white horse. Then the vultures came and ate their dead bodies.

"After this, I saw another angel come down from heaven with a key to the demonic pit and a large chain in his hand. He took hold of the dragon, the old serpent known as the devil, or Satan, tied him up, and confined him to his demonic pit for that 1,000 years. Then the angel locked the gate so the devil couldn't get away. After 1,000 years he will be released, but only for a little while (Rev. 19:17–20:3).

Trial by Jury

"During the 1,000 years the righteous were in heaven, sitting on thrones next to Jesus. Some were martyrs who had given their lives for Christ and for believing the Word of God. Others were there who had refused to worship the terrible animal and receive its mark.

"They are blessed, for they were raised at the first resurrection before the 1,000 years began and will not have to die again. They have the status of priests and were given power to judge for 1,000 years.

"All this time the wicked remained dead, but when the 1,000 years ended, they were brought back to life, and Satan was released from his confinement. When he saw the wicked who had been raised from the dead, he went all over the earth, gathering them together into an army so large they couldn't be counted. They came from all parts of the globe and surrounded the city of God, which had descended from heaven to earth.

"Then fire came down from heaven and destroyed them. The devil, who had deceived people into thinking they could overpower God, was also destroyed in that fire, along with the sea beast and the land animal who had become a false prophet. They were all destroyed forever (Rev. 20:4-10).

The Verdict

"Before Satan and his followers were destroyed, I saw God sitting on a great white throne. Heaven and earth seemed to melt at His presence. Those who had been dead, the great and the small, whether they had died at sea or been buried on land, stood before God. The books of heaven were opened, including the book of life. All people were judged by what was written in the books, according to what they had done.

"Anyone whose name was not in the book of life was destroyed by fire. Death and the grave came to an end. This is the second death, which is final (Rev. 20:11-15).

A New Beginning

"After this the scene changed, and I saw a new heaven and a new earth. The old earth with its atmosphere was gone, and so were the large oceans. I saw the city of God, the New Jerusalem, come down from heaven, looking as beautiful as a bride coming to meet her husband.

"I heard a voice from heaven say, 'Look! God has moved His

throne to earth to be with His people forever. They will be with Him, and He will be their God. He will wipe away all their tears, and there will be no more death or crying. And there will be no more pain, because the former things are passed away.'

"From His throne God's Son said, 'Look, I have made all things new. So write down what you've seen and heard, because it is true.' Then He said, 'It is done! I am the Alpha and the Omega, the Beginning and the End. The water of life is free. My people will inherit everything I promised. God will be their Father, and they will be His children.'

" 'But unbelievers, sinners, murderers, perverts, liars, traitors, the sexually immoral, and those who practiced magic and worshipped idols have died in the fire, which is the second death, and it will last forever' (Rev. 21:1-8).

The City

"Then one of the seven angels who had the seven bowls of God's judgment came over to me and said, 'Come, let me show you the city of God, the New Jerusalem, the bride of the Lamb.' He took me to a very high mountain. From there I could look down on the city of God, which had come from heaven and settled on the earth.

"The city was filled with light from the glory of God. It glistened like a precious gemstone as clear as crystal. It had beautiful, high walls with 12 gates going into the city and an angel at each gate. The names of the 12 tribes of Israel were on the gates, one name on each gate. There were three gates on each of the four sides of the city. The wall rested on 12 foundations, each of which was engraved with the name of one of the 12 apostles.

"The angel who showed me all this had a measuring stick in his hand, which he used to measure the city, including its foundations and walls. The city was laid out as a square and measured 1,500 miles on each side, and it was just as high as it was wide and long. The walls were made of precious stones, and the entire city was made of gold, as clear as crystal.

"The 12 foundations were made of 12 colored gemstones, a different color for each foundation. The 12 gates were made of 12 pearls, each gate of just one pearl. The streets of the city were made of gold, but as clear as glass.

"There was no need for a temple in the city as there had been in Jerusalem, because God and the Lamb are there in person. The city doesn't have to be lighted by the sun during the day or by the moon at night, because God and the Lamb are its light.

"The saved from all nations will live in that city and will give all the glory to God and to the Lamb. The gates will never close, because dark nights never come. No thieves, liars, or immoral persons will be there—only those whose names are written in the Lamb's book of life.

"Then the angel took me inside the city and showed me the river of life. Its water is as clear as crystal, flowing through the city, coming from the throne of God and the Lamb. In the middle of the city is the tree of life. The river flows around it, and its branches reach to both sides of the river. Each month it produces new fruit, and those who eat it will live forever.

"The curse of sin is gone. The throne of God and the Lamb is there. The people see God and talk with Him face to face. They all have the Father's name and gladly serve Him.

"There is no need of lights in the city, because of God's presence. From there, His people will govern the universe with Him forever (Rev. 21:9–22:5).

Final Message

"Then the angel said to me, 'Everything I've told you is true!' Just as God sent His angel to speak to the prophets of old, so He sent His angel to me, to show me what will soon take place.

"Jesus said to me, 'I will come quickly. Blessed are those who hold on to the prophecies written in this book.'

"I, John, am the one who saw and heard all these things. So I fell on my knees in gratitude before the angel who showed me these things. He said, 'Stand up! I'm one of God's servants, just as you are and as the prophets were and as those are who believe what's written in this book. Don't worship me. Worship God!'

"Then he said, 'Don't seal the prophecies of this book, because those who live at the end of earth's history will need them. The time will come when those who are unjust will not change, and those who are morally filthy will remain that way. But let those who do right continue to do right, and those who are holy continue to be holy.'

"Then Jesus said, 'I will come quickly and will reward everyone according to what he has done. I am the Alpha and the Omega, the First and the Last, the Beginning and the End. Blessed are those whose sins are washed away and who keep My commandments. They have the right to enter the city and eat from the tree of life. Outside are liars, murderers, those who practice magic, the sexually immoral, and idol worshipers.

"'I sent My angel to tell you these things so that you can write them down and send them to the churches. I am the Foundation Stone and the Offspring of the house of David. I am the Bright Morning Star!'

"The Holy Spirit says to everyone, 'Come!' The churches say, 'Come!' Let those who hear this message say, 'Come! Whoever is thirsty, come and drink the water of life. It's free!'

"I, John, warn everyone who hears the prophecies of this book not to add anything contrary to them. If anyone does, God will add to his punishment the full weight of judgment described in this book. If anyone takes away from these prophecies, God will take away his right to the city and to the tree of life.

"Jesus says, 'When I come, I will come quickly!'

"Yes, come, Lord Jesus! Come quickly! The grace of the Lord Jesus Christ be with all of you. Amen" (Rev. 22:6-21).